BOSS BABIES

An Entrepreneur Alphabet Book for Future Bosses

By
Daryl Giles

A BlackEve Media Production
(www.BlackEveMedia.com)

To Contact Author please use the following mediums:
BossBabiesBook@gmail.com

IN
DEDICATION
TO

I wrote this book
for my son &
decided to give it
to the world.. 🌍

- D.GILES

66

INSPIRED

BY

After reading the Wright Twins' Promise to A, B, C's children's book, it inspired me to create a book for my son.

- D.GILES

IN

66

REMEMBERENCE

OF

One of my childhood best friends, Michael "Mike Mike" White... until we meet again.

- D.GILES

A

ASSETS

Assets put money ($) in your pockets

Assets have value

ACTION

Action is doing something to achieve a goal

Action concurs fear

ACCOUNTABILITY

Accountability is taking responsibility for your actions

B

BALANCE SHEET

Balance sheet can be an X-ray of the financial condition of a company

Balance sheet shows Assets vs. liabilities

BELIEVE

When you believe, you release creative powers

BONDS

The highest rating issued is AAA, AA, A
High Quality B's, C's

CREATIVITY

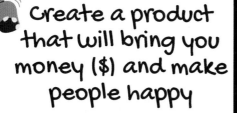

Create a product that will bring you money ($) and make people happy

CREDIT

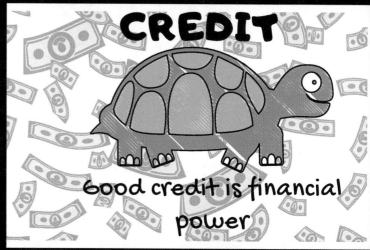

Good credit is financial power

COURAGE

Have the courage to be your own constructive critic. Seek out all flaws and correct them

CRITICAL THINKING

Analyzing and evaluating a situation & coming to the best solution

D

DEFENSIVE STOCKS

Stock of companies that sell goods & services that are needed like food & utilities

DIVIDENDS

Payments from a company to their share/stock holders

DEDICATION

To be devoted to a task of a purpose

E

EDUCATION

$2+2=4$

Education before compensation

EXERCISE

You have to exercise your mind, body, & soul daily

EQUITY

The value of shares you own in a company

F

FINANCIAL FREEDOM

The ability to make your money ($) make more money ($$$)

You reach financial freedom when you never have to do something that you do not want to because of a lack of money

GENERATIONAL WEALTH

Assets that you can leave to your kids
and grandkids

H

HEART

Unwavering courage

HUSTLE

Without hustle, your talent will only get you

I

INVEST

Is the science of money ($) making money ($$)

INTEGRITY

The quality of being honest and have strong morals & principals

INTEREST

Extra money you have to pay back for borrowed money ($)

J

JOINT ACCOUNT

If you get a joint account with your mom/dad you'll have access to their money.

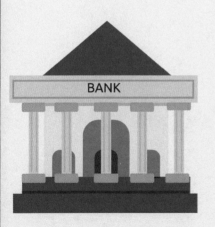  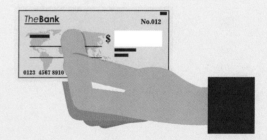

K

KNOWLEDGE

Understanding that it is not about what you know when you start a business it's about what you learn and put into use after you opened your business

L

Life Insurance

A policy that provides money ($) to your family once you die providing Generational wealth.

LLC

Limited liability Company — something you'll need when starting your business

Liabilities

The bills you have to pay (money that leaves pockets, monthly)

M

Master Mind Group

A group of 4 — 5 people that come together as a team and make each other better

Marketing

Promoting and advertising the product or services you're selling.

Mutual Funds

To invest in a collection of companies from different sectors, industries, and market caps.

N

Negotiation

Bargaining process between 2 people seeking to come to a mutual/reasonable agreement.

Make the offer fair 2 where yall both win and people will love doing business with you.

Ownership

Having possession of something that you can pass down through inheritance, increasing generational wealth

Operating System

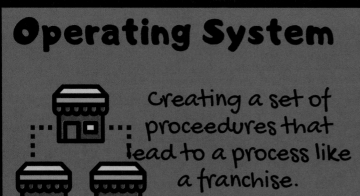

Creating a set of proceedures that lead to a process like a franchise.

Obstacles

Things that may go wrong, but you should never quit.

P

Passive Income

Money ($) recieved without any work being done

Plan

The moves you make should be focused around the context of the plan

Profit

Money ($) you get to keep after you pay all expenses

Q

Quality

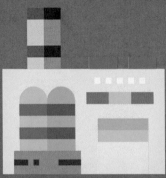

The standard of something as measured against other things of a similar kind.

To produce something of excellence.

R

Rat Race

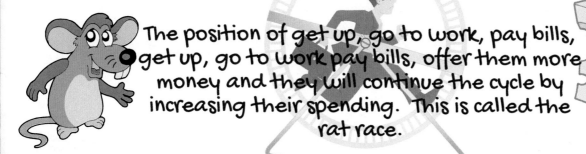

The position of get up, go to work, pay bills, get up, go to work pay bills, offer them more money and they will continue the cycle by increasing their spending. This is called the rat race.

Real Estate

Property, land, and buildings

Rich

If you want to be rich you must know the difference between an asset and a liability, and buy assets.

S

Supply & Demand

The relationship between what's available (the supply) and what people want and is willing to pay for them (the demand)

Salary

Money earned by working for someone else. If your salary is your only source of income, your 1st step away from poverty

Self-Discipline

The ability to control your feelings and overcome your weaknesses

Transportation/ Trucking

1 of the Biggest Industries in America. If those trucks stop this country will stop!

Tax Breaks

A tax break can come in the form of claiming deductions or excluding income from your tax return.

U

Understanding

Sympathetically aware of other peoples feeling tolerant and forgiving.
"Don't be in such a hurry to condemn a man because he doesn't think as you think. It was a time when you didn't know what you know today."
-Malcolm X

V

Value

A person's principles and ones judgement of what's important in life.

Vision

Big thinkers train themselves to see not only what is, but also what can be) (seeing 5% with your eyes, 95% with your mind).

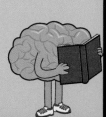

W

Wisdom

Have good judgment on things from experience and knowledge

Work Ethic

Hard work builds character, fast success builds ego.

A Nasdaq stock symbol specifying that it is a mutual fund.
A symbol used in stock transaction tables to indicate that a stock is trading ex-dividends or ex-rights.

Year Plan

Write down your Year Plan at the beginning of the year, by the end of the year you should be completed at least 80% of your 1yr plan.

Z

Zero Down

When you have good credit you'll get a lot of stuff with no-money-down.

Made in the USA
Columbia, SC
30 September 2020